5/09

Danica Patrick

By Jeff Savage

AMAZING ATHLETES

Lerner Publications Company • Minneapolis

Lerner Publications Company
A division of Lerner Publishing Group, Inc.
241 First Avenue North
Minneapolis, MN 55401 U.S.A.

Website address: www.lernerbooks.com

Library of Congress Cataloging-in-Publication Data

Savage, Jeff, 1961–
    Danica Patrick / by Jeff Savage.
        p.   cm. — (Amazing athletes)
    Includes index.
    ISBN-13: 978–0–8225–5954–2 (lib. bdg. : alk. paper)
    ISBN-10: 0–8225–5954–4 (lib. bdg. : alk. paper)
    1. Patrick, Danica, 1982–Juvenile literature. 2. Automobile racing drivers—United States—Biography—Juvenile literature. 3. Women automobile racing drivers—United States—Biography—Juvenile literature. I. Title. II. Series.
    GV1032.P38S38 2007
    796.72092—dc22   2005037288

Manufactured in the United States of America
3 4 5 6 7 8 – DP – 12 11 10 09 08 07

Table of Contents

Danica rounds turn one in her number 16 car at her first Indianapolis 500 on May 29, 2005.

A FAST START

Danica Patrick gripped the steering wheel. She swerved right, then left. Her car roared through traffic at 225 miles per hour. Danica was racing against the world's best Indy car drivers in the 2005 Indianapolis 500.

Danica was the only woman competing in the race. In fact, she was only the fourth woman ever to drive in the race.

Danica was in 16th place when she made her move. She sped around the track, passing one car after another. By **lap** 155, she had moved into fourth place. Only 45 laps to go! Her heart was pounding. Her stomach was in knots. But she was confident and focused.

The Indianapolis 500 race is a 500-mile race held every year at Indianapolis Motor Speedway in Indianapolis, Indiana. The race goes for 200 laps, or 200 times around the track.

Then trouble struck. The cars in front of her slowed suddenly. Danica hit the brakes. Her car went into a spin, and she bashed into another car.

Danica's car *(left)* spins while Tomas Scheckter hits the brakes of his car to avoid her.

She was forced to go to the **pits** for repairs. The Rahal Letterman Racing **crew** went to work. Danica was soon back on the track with new tires and more fuel. But she had dropped to ninth place.

Just 28 laps remained in the race when another crash hit. Car parts scattered across the track. The eight drivers in front of Danica went to the pits for fuel. But Danica and her crew decided to take a chance. They thought her car might have enough fuel to finish the race. She stayed on the track. On the **restart** two laps later, Danica rocketed ahead and into the lead! Nearly 300,000 people at Indianapolis Motor Speedway were on their feet cheering. Danica was the first woman ever to lead the famous race.

The Rahal Letterman Racing crew works on Danica's car in the pits.

Around and around the oval track she went. Just 18 laps to go . . . 17 . . . 16. The crowd screamed louder. Danica was a small 5-foot 2-inch, 100-pound **rookie.** This was her first year in racing. She was competing in only her fifth **Indy Racing League** (IRL) event.

The crowd cheers as Danica roars past another car and into the lead.

Danica was 23 years old when she became the fourth woman to compete in the Indianapolis 500. Janet Guthrie was 39 when she competed in 1977. Lyn St. James was 45. Sarah Fisher was 19.

With just 14 laps to go, **veteran** Dan Wheldon nosed ahead of her. Danica wanted the lead back. She radioed her pit crew to ask if she could use the overtake button on her steering wheel. The button gives the car a boost of speed. But it uses lots of fuel.

Crew engineer Ray Leto told her to try it. Danica hit the button and blew past Wheldon and into the lead. The crowd roared. Just 10 laps remained. "Wow, I can actually win this," Danica thought. But Danica's car was dangerously low on fuel. Could she keep the lead?

Karting is a popular sport around the world. Danica raced against other kids her age in karts like these.

CATCHING ON

Danica Sue Patrick was born March 25, 1982, in Beloit, Wisconsin. She grew up in the town of Roscoe in northern Illinois. Her father, T.J., was a champion snowmobile racer. Her mother, Bev, was a car mechanic. The two had met at a snowmobile race.

Danica was not interested in cars as a young girl. She preferred playing with Barbie dolls. "She was a girlie girl," said her mother. "She didn't want to get grease under her fingernails."

When Danica was 10, her younger sister Brooke asked to try driving a **go-kart**. Danica decided to go too. In her first attempt at driving, Danica swerved to miss a truck in the parking lot and crashed head-on into a concrete wall. Fortunately, she was wearing her seat belt and helmet. She was not hurt.

Soon Danica got the hang of driving the karts. "I loved the way you could see yourself get better in racing," said Danica. "I'd go around the track in maybe 52 seconds. I'd come in and ask my dad. 'Was that 51?' Then I'd say, 'OK, let's do 50. Let's do 49, 48. Seeing the improvement was so satisfying."

A few months later, Brooke crashed four times in one race. She gave up go-karting. But Danica was hooked. Before long, she had broken the track record at Sugar River Raceway in southern Wisconsin.

In 1993, Danica began competing in **World Karting Association** (WKA) events. She finished fourth in one series of races and second in another. Some boys and their parents were jealous. Danica understood. "No dad wants his boy beaten by a little girl," she said. But plenty of boys lost to Danica. A year later, she

Like Danica, many of the world's great race car drivers grew up racing go-karts. They include four-time NASCAR champion Jeff Gordon, two-time NASCAR champion Tony Stewart, and seven-time Formula One World Champion Michael Schumacher.

About 100,000 Americans enjoy the sport of karting on race tracks. Go-karts are about 6 feet long and 4 feet wide. They weigh about 150 pounds. Kids can begin racing karts at age five.

won her first national points championship. She won more titles in 1995 and 1996.

Danica was also active at Hononegah High School. She was a cheerleader and played volleyball and basketball. She sang in the school choir and played flute in the band. But her true passion was racing. In 1996, she competed in 49 races. She won 39 of them! "But it was never good enough," she told herself. "I could always be better."

Danica in front of her Formula Vauxhall car in Great Britain in 1998.

Going Places

Danica dared to be great. At the age of 14, she took a course taught by former Indy 500 driver Lyn St. James. She learned to eat healthy foods and how to concentrate while racing. St. James was impressed with her young student. "She was talented, committed, and poised," said St. James.

When Danica turned 16, she was invited to race in the Formula Vauxhall Series in Europe. She would race against other young drivers in small, lightweight race cars. With her parents' permission, she quit school during her **junior year** in high school. She moved alone to Milton Keynes, England.

"England is a great place for racing. It was my college," said Danica. Her only regret was not graduating from high school with her classmates. But she did get her **GED (general equivalency diploma).** In Great Britain, Danica stayed with her friends and slept on the living room couch for two months. Then she moved into a tiny bedroom the size of a closet.

Danica races in a Formula Vauxhall Series event in 1998 while in Great Britain.

Danica lived and breathed racing. Her hard work paid off. In just her first full year, she finished an amazing ninth in the Vauxhall **points standings**. But some of the male drivers did not welcome her. They didn't like competing against a girl. And they really didn't like finishing races behind a girl. "It was boys being boys," said Danica. "I got really cold and just hard. I had to be. I had to get tough. It forced me to grow up very quickly."

Danica missed her family. She returned home to Roscoe from time to time. She enjoyed working at the family-owned Java Hut coffee shop.

Danica knows it is important to always work hard. "You can go from zero to hero and back again really fast," she says. "You have to keep moving. You have to keep thinking, 'I can be better.' You have to be persistent."

But after being away from the track for a few weeks, Danica would hurry back to Great Britain for more racing.

As Danica improved, she moved up into faster and tougher racing leagues. She dreamed of becoming a driver in a big-time league like the IRL or **Championship Auto Racing Teams (CART)**. But would a top-level racing team trust a woman to drive their race car?

Indy car legend Bobby Rahal
saw Danica's driving talent.

INTO THE BIG TIME

In 2000, Danica's performance caught the
attention of Bobby Rahal. Rahal was a former
CART champion and Indy 500 winner. He and
late-night TV star David Letterman owned the
Rahal Letterman Racing team.

Danica pushes her car to the limit during a Barber Dodge Pro Series race in 2002.

"There are lots of talented drivers," Rahal said. "But few make the sacrifices that Danica has. She is serious enough to do whatever it takes." In 2002, Rahal offered Danica a three-year **contract** to drive a car for his team. Danica eagerly accepted.

Rahal told Danica that if she worked hard, she would get a chance to race in the IRL. But first, Danica raced in the 2002 **Barber Dodge Pro Series**. This was a circuit where young drivers developed their skills. In her first race in Toronto, she finished a very good seventh.

Three weeks later in Vancouver, she did even better, finishing fourth.

In 2003, Danica moved up to the next level, the **Toyota Atlantic Series**. At the Monterrey Grand Prix in Mexico, she finished third and became the first woman to earn a place on the **podium**. In the season finale in Miami, she finished a season-best second. For the year, she ranked sixth in overall points.

Josh Hunt's car crashes over Danica's car during a 2004 Toyota Atlantic Series race.

Danica was working harder than ever. She ran nearly five miles each day. She strengthened her body with weight training. She ate only healthy foods, especially fish, fruits, and vegetables. She drank plenty of her favorite beverage—water. In 2004, she finished in the top five in 10 of the 12 races she entered. She was the only driver to complete every lap of every race. She was ready to compete against some of the world's best drivers in the IRL.

By 2002, Danica had become very popular. Young girls gave her handmade bracelets. Male college students lined up to pose for pictures with her.

Danica looks serious as she prepares for the 2005 Indianapolis 500.

MAKING AN IMPACT

The night before Danica drove her first Indy car, she barely slept. "I woke up about every 20 minutes," she said. "I realized there's no joking anymore." But when Danica actually drove the powerful car, she soon saw that she could control it. In her fourth IRL race, in Montegi, Japan, she finished an impressive fourth.

Danica *(top)* is confident on the racetrack. But she doesn't take unnecessary chances.

Then came the Indianapolis 500. Nearly three hours into the race, with 10 laps left, Danica found herself in the lead! The crowd roared as Danica went around the oval track again and again. Unfortunately, she was nearly out of fuel. She did not want to stop on the track and have all the cars pass her. She had to slow down. With six laps left, Dan Wheldon passed her. Then Vitor Meira passed her. Bryan Herta zipped by too. Danica crossed the finish line in fourth place.

Danica was disappointed with herself. "I lost the lead," she thought. "I didn't win." But then she saw the huge smiles and tears of joy on the faces of her pit crew and family. She realized all she had done. "I got to lead my first Indy 500. I actually had a chance to win the race," she said. "I accomplished a lot."

David Letterman, co-owner of the Rahal Letterman team, congratulates Danica at the 2005 Indy 500.

Danica's performance made headlines in newspapers across the country. Her picture appeared on the cover of *Sports Illustrated* magazine. It was the first time an Indy 500 driver had been on the cover in 20 years. "DanicaMania" swept the country. Sales of Danica hats, key chains, and other products went through the roof. Reporters swarmed Danica. "I try not to get too overwhelmed by the media attention," she said. "But this is great. We have made an impact!"

Danica is swarmed with reporters before and after every race.

Danica poses with her Rahal Letterman team. It takes an entire team to win an Indy car race.

Danica raced well the rest of the year and had several strong finishes, but she did not capture a win. That was normal. Only one rookie in the last 10 years has actually won a race. Everyone in racing knows it takes practice. "As long as we keep working hard, the wins will come," says Danica.

In the meantime, companies have asked Danica to **sponsor** their products. She receives millions of dollars to **endorse** cars, furniture, and clothes. Even Danica did not know she would create such craziness. "I've always raced against the guys and I just see myself as one of them," she says. "I'm just a racer who happens to be a woman. At the end of the day, when I take my helmet off, I'm still a girl."

Danica and Paul Hospenthal arrive at the ESPY Awards in 2005. Danica and Paul married in November 2005.

Selected Career Highlights

2007   Finished eighth at Indianapolis 500

2006   Signed deal to drive for Andretti Green Racing in 2007
Published autobiography titled *Danica: Crossing the Line*

2005   Finished fourth at Indianapolis 500
Named IRL Rookie of the Year

2004   Finished third in Toyota Atlantic Series Championship with 269 points
Had 10 top-five finishes in 12 races
Only driver in Atlantic 12-race series to complete every lap
Became first female driver to win pole position in Toyota Atlantic Series at Round 5 at Portland, Oregon

2003   Finished sixth in Toyota Atlantic Series Championship with 269 points
Had 5 top-five finishes in 12 races
Became first female to post a podium (top three) result in 30-year history of Toyota Atlantic Series at Monterrey, Mexico

2002   Captured the pole and won the Toyota Pro/Celebrity Race at the Long Beach Grand Prix
Finished seventh in first Barber Dodge Pro Series event at Toronto
Finished fourth at Vancouver for her highest finish

2001   Won the Gorsline Scholarship Award for the top upcoming road racing driver

2000   Finished second at Formula Ford Festival in Great Britain, the highest-ever finish for an American in 26 years

1999   Finished ninth in Formula Vauxhall Championship in Great Britain

1998   Made debut in Great Britain at the age of 16 in Formula Vauxhall Series

1997   Won World Karting Association (WKA) Grand National Championship HPV class
Won WKA Grand National Championship in Yamaha Lite class

1996   Won 39 of 49 karting races

Glossary

Barber Dodge Pro Series: Formerly CART's third circuit. In this league, drivers competed in identical cars. Pro Series racers hoped to move up to CART's next level, the Toyota Atlantic Series.

Championship Auto Racing Teams (CART): Formerly the top American open-wheel racing league. CART became the Champ Car World Series in 2004.

contract: a written agreement

crew: the members of a racing team who build and repair the cars

crew engineer: the main crew member in charge of the engine of the car

endorse: to show support or approval of a product

GED (general equivalency diploma): a certificate that can serve as a high school diploma

go-kart: a small, flat, one-person vehicle with a motor. Go-karts are used for racing (called karting).

Indy Racing League: One of the top (with the Champ Car World Series) American-based open-wheel racing leagues. Indy cars race on oval and road tracks across the United States.

junior year: third of four years in high school or college

lap: a complete trip around a racetrack

pits: the area (also called pit row) along the track where cars stop for fuel and repairs

podium: the platform on which the top-three finishers in a race stand to receive their awards

points standings: a list that shows how many points each driver has earned. Points are awarded based on place of finish. The driver with the most points is at the top of the list.

restart: A start that comes after a race delay following a crash. A green flag is waved to resume racing.

rookie: a first-year player or driver in a sport or league

sponsor: to represent a product or company in exchange for money

Toyota Atlantic Series: Formerly CART's second circuit. Toyota Atlantic Series drivers hope to earn a spot in one of the sport's top circuits, such as the Indy Racing League.

veteran: a racer who has competed for several years

World Karting Association: the main organization that oversees go-kart races

Further Reading & Websites

Fish, Bruce. *Indy-Car Racing*. Philadelphia: Chelsea House Publishers, 2006.

Raby, Philip. *Racing Cars*. Minneapolis: LernerSports, 1999.

Stewart, Mark. *Auto Racing: A History of Fast Cars and Fearless Drivers*. New York: Franklin Watts Publishers, 1998.

Danica's Website
http://www.danicaracing.com
Danica's official website features trivia, photos, records, and information about Danica, her race car, and the IRL.

Indy Racing League
http://www.indyracing.com
The IRL's website provides fans with recent news stories, statistics, schedules, and biographies of drivers and teams.

Sports Illustrated for Kids
http://www.sikids.com
The *Sports Illustrated for Kids* website covers all sports, including auto racing.

World Karting Association
http://www.worldkarting.com/
Learn more about the fun and exciting sport of go-kart racing from the official site of the World Karting Association.

Index

Photo Acknowledgments

The photos in this book are used with the permission of:

Mark Cowan/Icon SMI, p. 4, 29; AP/Wide World Photos, pp. 6, 25; AJ Mast/Icon SMI, pp. 7, 8, 19; © Alexander Hubrich/zefa/CORBIS, p. 10; Sutton-Images.com, pp. 14, 16, 21; © Darrell Ingham/Getty Images, p. 20; © Robert Mora/Getty Images, p. 22; © Jeff Roberts/AFP/Getty Images, p. 23; © Gavin Lawrence/Getty Images, pp. 24, 26, 27; © Frazer Harrison/Getty Images, p. 28.

Front Cover: © David Bailey/ZUMA Press.